Date ____________

Larger or smaller?

You need:

- red and ye

Compare numbers

0	1	2	3	4			7		9			12				16		18		

Teacher's notes

Look at the numbers on each pair of doors and decide which of the two numbers is larger. Colour the larger number yellow and the smaller number red. Then complete the 0–20 number track underneath.

More or less balloons

- Compare and order numbers to 30

You need:
- red and yellow coloured pencils

Teacher's notes

In each set, colour the balloon with the larger number yellow, and the balloon with the smaller number red. In the middle balloon, write a number that lies between them.

Activity Book 1C

Collins

New Primary Maths

1

Date ____________________

Balloon race

Write numbers to 30

one ten
and
nine units

I ten
and
five ones

2 tens
and
4 units

2 tens
and
nine units

two 10s
and
one unit

three tens
and
no units

	16	17	18		20		22	23		25	26	27	28		

Teacher's notes

Read the tens and units information on each hot air balloon and write the corresponding number on the basket underneath. Then write each number in the number track at the bottom.

Tenmorethan Town

Say the number that is 10 more than a given number

Teacher's notes

Match each person's shorts to the colour of the front door on their house. Then look at the number on their top. Write the number that is 10 more on their house.

Date ____________________

Tenlessthan Town

Say the number that is 10 less than a given number

Teacher's notes

Match each person's shorts to the colour of the front door on their house. Then look at the number on their top. Write the number that is 10 less on their house.

Add on ten!

- Say the number that is 10 more than a given number

You need:

- coloured pencils

1	2	3	4	5	6	7	8	9	10
11	12	13	14	15	16	17	18	19	20
21	22	23	24	25	26	27	28	29	30
31	32	33	34	35	36	37	38	39	40
41	42	43	44	45	46	47	48	49	50

5 + 10 = ☐　　☐ + 10 = ☐

☐ + 10 = ☐　　☐ + 10 = ☐

☐ + 10 = ☐　　☐ + 10 = ☐

☐ + 10 = ☐　　☐ + 10 = ☐

Teacher's notes

Look at each coloured number on the number square, and add on 10, colouring the answer to match. Then complete each calculation as an addition number sentence in the boxes.

Date ______________________

Mountain addition

Add more than two numbers

$7 + 2 + 1 =$ 10	$6 + 5 + 3 =$ 14
$5 + 3 + 4 =$ ☐	$9 + 4 + 3 =$ ☐
$6 + 4 + 1 =$ ☐	$5 + 10 + 4 =$ ☐
$7 + 2 + 5 =$ ☐	$2 + 9 + 7 =$ ☐
$10 + 1 + 2 =$ ☐	$3 + 5 + 12 =$ ☐
$3 + 9 + 3 =$ ☐	$4 + 5 + 8 =$ ☐

Teacher's notes

Complete each addition calculation and write the answer in the boxes.

Take off ten!

- Say the number that is 10 less than a given number

You need:

- coloured pencils

1	2	3	4	5	6	7	8	9	10
11	12	13	14	15	16	17	18	19	20
21	22	23	24	25	26	27	28	29	30
31	32	33	34	35	36	37	38	39	40
41	42	43	44	45	46	47	48	49	50

13 – 10 = ☐ ☐ – 10 = ☐

☐ – 10 = ☐ ☐ – 10 = ☐

☐ – 10 = ☐ ☐ – 10 = ☐

☐ – 10 = ☐ ☐ – 10 = ☐

Teacher's notes

Look at each coloured number on the number square, and take away 10, colouring the answer to match. Then complete each calculation as a subtraction number sentence in the boxes.

Patterns of nine

- **Know addition and subtraction facts for 9**

Teacher's notes

In each row of windows, solve the addition and subtraction calculations for 9 by writing in the correct number.

Doubles and halves

Solve word problems

Leo had 12 dinosaurs.

He gave half of them to Caie.

How many dinosaurs did Leo give to Caie?

Skateboard Stickers cost 7p each.

Cavan bought two stickers.

How much did Cavan spend on skateboard stickers?

Ayesha had 10 charms on her bracelet. That was only half of her collection!

How many charms did Ayesha have altogether?

Lucy had 20 sweets. That was double the number that Naomi had.

How many sweets did Naomi have?

Teacher's notes

Look at each problem in turn and decide whether it is a 'double' or 'halve' problem. Find the answer and write it in the space provided. Use the space underneath each problem to show how you worked it out.

Date ____________________

Crazy paving patterns

You need:

- coloured pencils

- **Continue patterns involving 2-D shapes**

Teacher's notes

Look at each pattern. Then draw the correct shapes in the spaces and colour them to complete each pattern correctly.

Date ____________________

Railway track shapes

- Describe features of 2-D shapes

You need:

- blue, orange, and yellow coloured pencils

Teacher's notes

Look at the shapes on each railway track. Colour the shapes with straight sides only, blue; with curved sides only, orange; with both straight and curved sides, yellow. Now colour the train to match.

Date ______________________

Building site blocks

- Continue patterns involving 3-D solids

Teacher's notes

Look at each solid shape pattern and then draw a line to match the correct shape needed to complete each sequence correctly.

Date ____________________

Dredger edges

- **Recognise features of common 3–D solids**

You need:

- red, green and blue coloured pencils

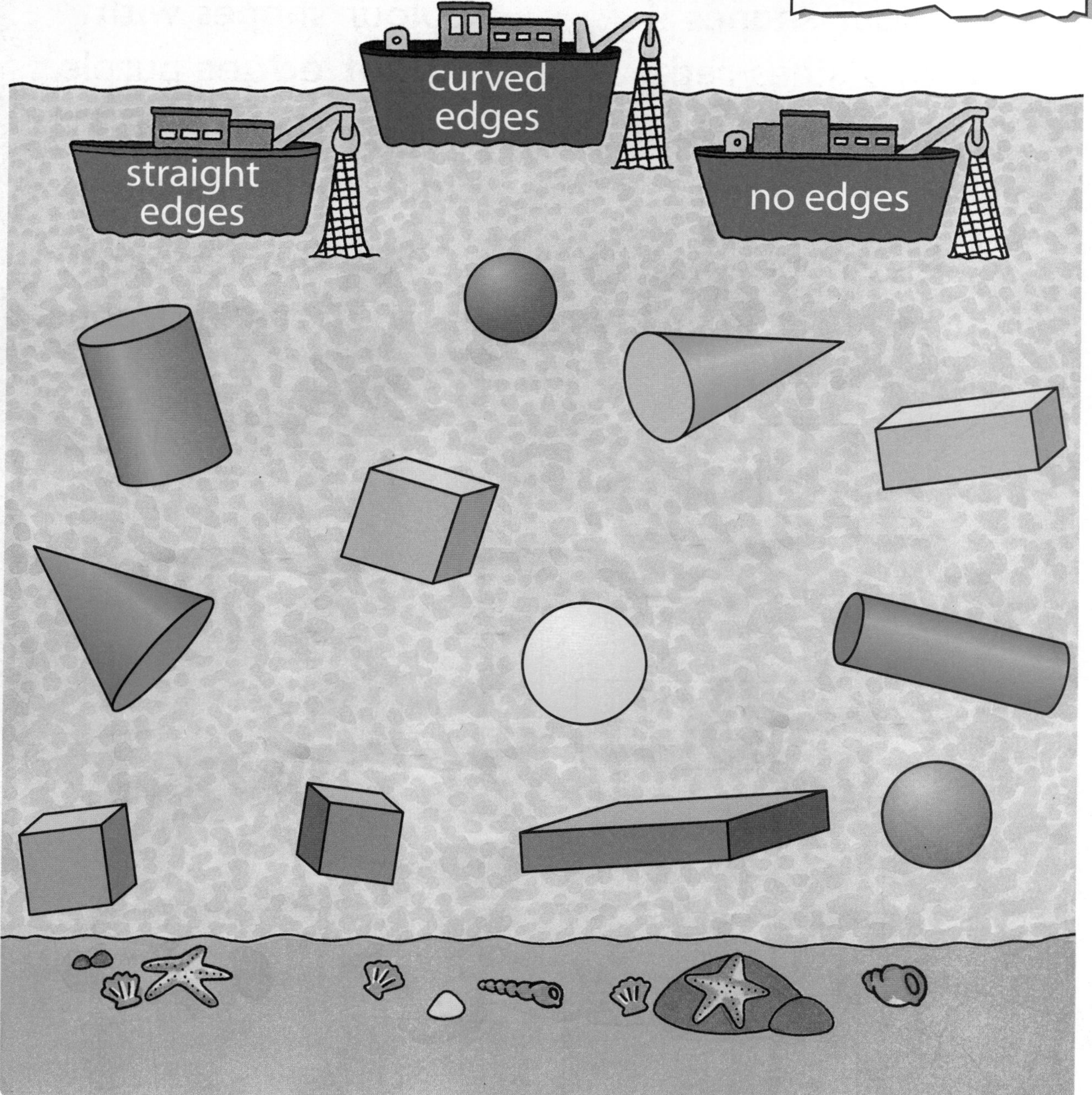

Teacher's notes

Each dredger collects a different kind of shape. Using the same colour as each dredger, draw a line to connect the dredger with the shape it is collecting.

Date ____________________

Shape sorter

- Recognise features of common 2-D and 3-D shapes

You need:

- coloured pencils

Colour shapes with **3** sides red.

Colour shapes with **4** sides green.

Circle shapes with **straight sides** in yellow.

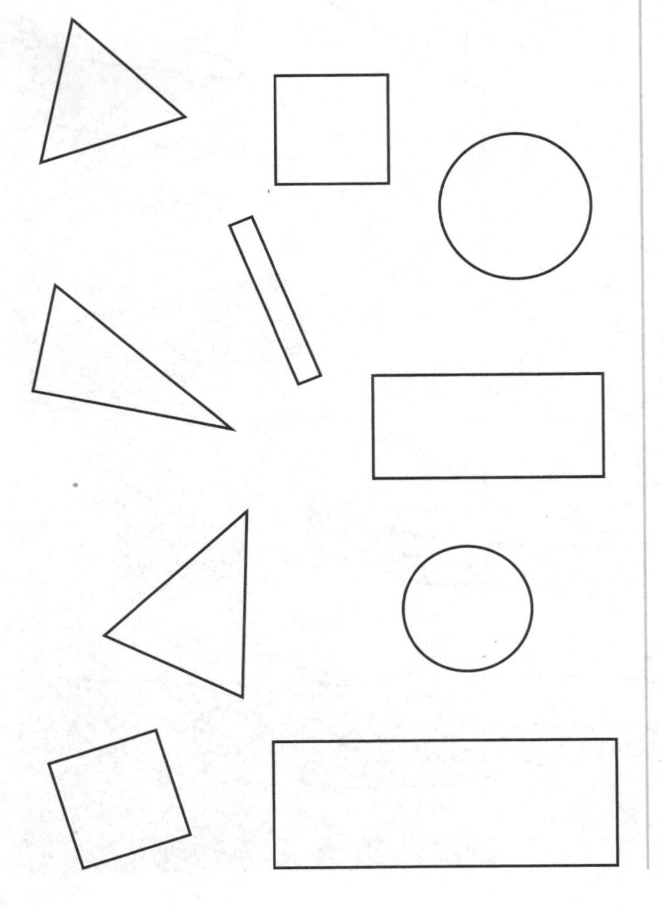

Colour shapes with **straight edges** purple.

Colour shapes with **circular faces** blue.

Circle shapes with **curved faces** in orange.

Teacher's notes

In each section, read the instructions to sort the shapes by colouring or circling them in the appropriate colour.

Date ___________________

Parachute addition

You need:

- coloured pencils

Add two numbers

0	1	2	3	4	5	6	7	8	9	10	11	12	13	14	15	16	17	18	19	20	21	22	23	24	25

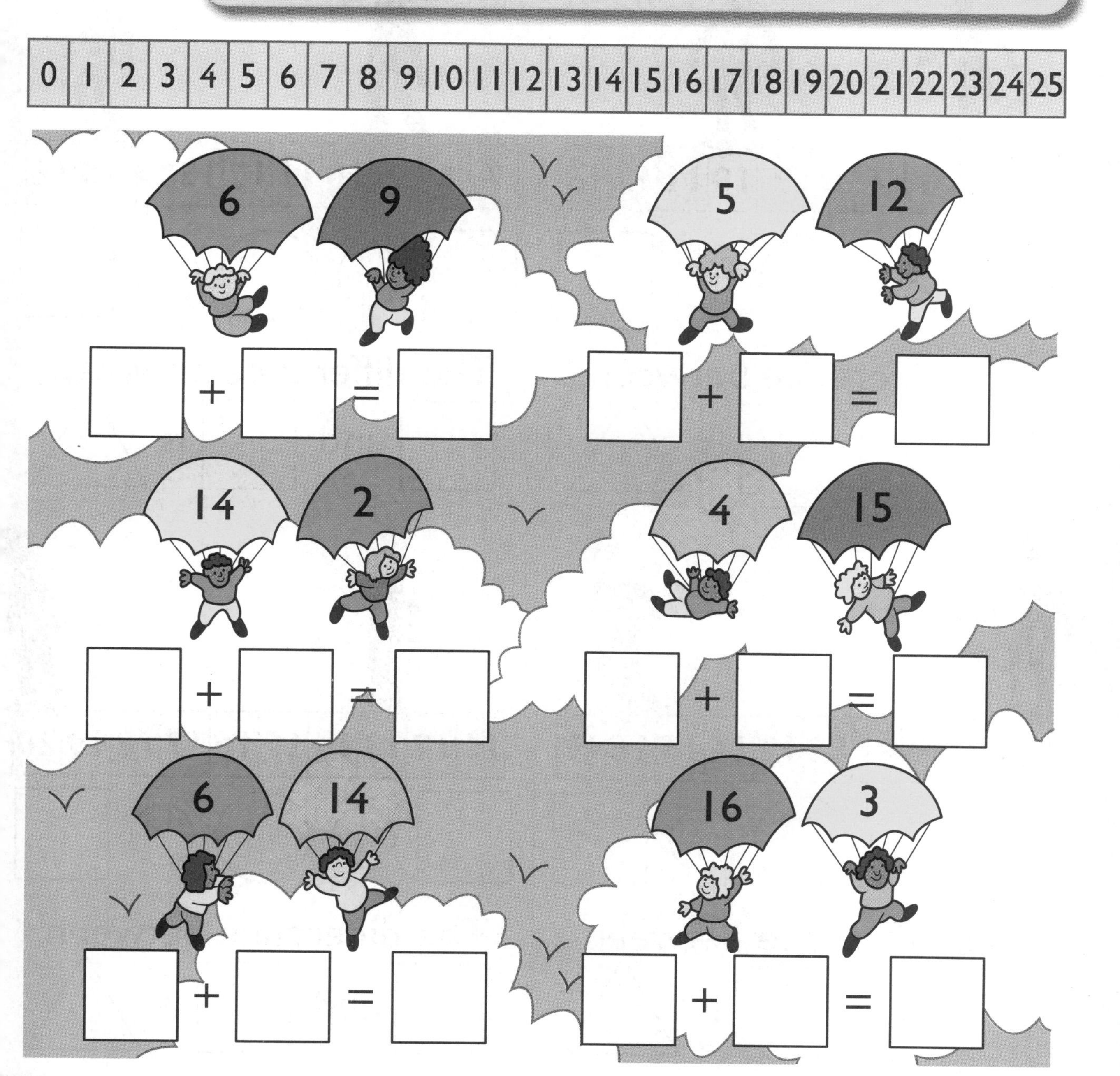

Teacher's notes

Look at the numbers on each pair of parachutes. Write the numbers as an addition calculation, starting with the larger number first. Then show the jumps on the number track, using a different colour for each calculation. Then complete each calculation by writing the answer in the box.

Date ______________________

Skateboard subtraction

Understand subtraction as finding a difference

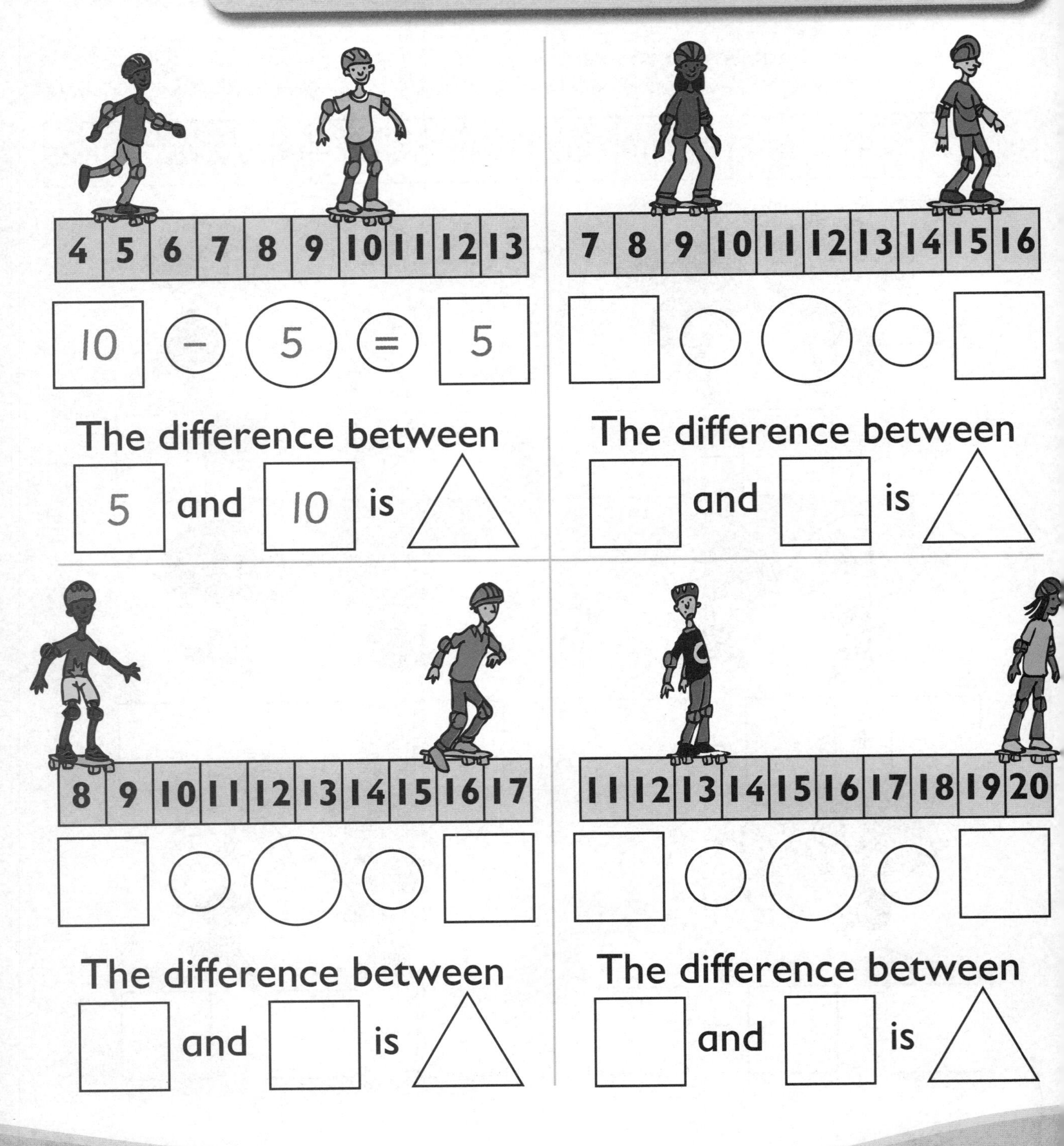

Teacher's notes

Look at the position of each skater and find the difference between them. Write this as a calculation underneath and then complete the sentence.

Date ____________________

Adding and subtracting starships

- Add and subtract pairs of numbers

You need:
- coloured pencils

Teacher's notes

Look at the addition or subtraction calculation on each starship. Find the star which shows the correct number to complete the calculation. Then colour the starship to match the star.

Date ____________________

Exploring planet 9

- Know addition and subtraction facts

Teacher's notes

Trace the route of each alien to its spaceship and find the number which, when added to the alien, makes a total of 9. Write this number on the spaceship.

Date ____________________

Chilly problems

Solve number problems

Teacher's notes

In each row, write three numbers which, when added together, make 15. Use the penguins to help you.

Date ____________

Double bass doubles

- **Know doubles of all numbers to at least 10**

3 + 3 = 6	☐ + ☐ = ☐	☐ + ☐ = ☐

☐ + ☐ = ☐	☐ + ☐ = ☐	☐ + ☐ = ☐

Teacher's notes

Look at each pair of double bass musicians. Use the numbers on their instruments to write an addition double and its total in the space underneath.

Date ____________________

How many candles?

Use doubles to work out other addition calculations

Teacher's notes

Work out the sum on each cake and draw the correct number of candles. Draw a line from each cake to the balloon which gives the matching calculation.

Date ____________________

Pot plant addition

Recognise that addition can be done in any order

You need:

- coloured pencils

Teacher's notes

Left-hand column: Write the appropriate numbers on each pair of pots and complete the addition calculation.
Right-hand column: Repeat. Then find the differently-ordered matching pair in the left-hand column and draw a line to match it with the calculation in the right-hand column.

Pirate ship tens

- Know pairs of numbers that total 10

You need:

- red coloured pencil

Teacher's notes

Work out the addition calculation on each pirate ship. If the calculation shows a pair of numbers with a total of 10, colour the ship's flag in red and draw a line to join it to Treasure Island.

Date ____________________

Calculation rescue

- Know addition and subtraction facts

Teacher's notes

Look at the addition calculation on each tower, colour its flag and turret to match the shield showing the correct total. Look at the subtraction calculations on the horses and find the related subtraction fact for each addition fact. Draw a line between the matching horse and tower.

Date ____________

Full or empty?

- Understand words related to capacity

You need:
- coloured pencils

almost full

full

almost full

empty

full

full

empty

almost full

full

full

Teacher's notes

Draw and colour the contents of each container to match its label.

Date ____________________

More or less capacity

You need:
- coloured pencils

Understand words related to capacity

A cup holds less than a

A bucket holds more than a

A big box holds more than a

A purse holds less than a

A jar holds less than a

Teacher's notes

Draw objects which can hold more or less than the objects illustrated.

Date ____________________

Fill them up

- Estimate capacities

little spoon

cup

jug

big spoon

bucket

about ☐ cups full

about ☐ cups full

about ☐ big spoons full

about ☐ cups full

about ☐ buckets full

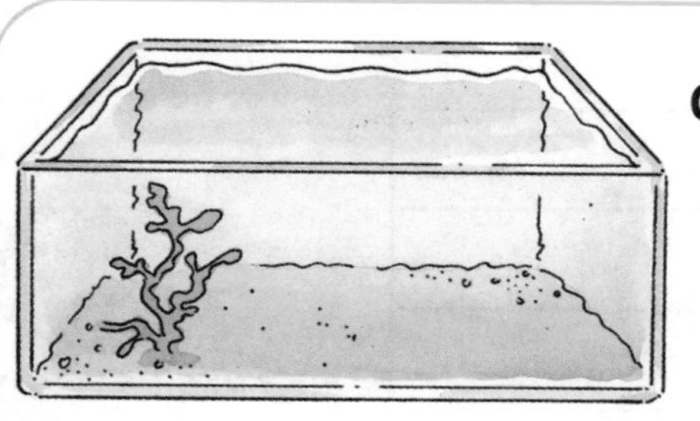

about ☐ jugs full

about ☐ little spoons full

about ☐ big spoons full

Teacher's notes

Look at the containers at the top. Estimate haw many of each it will take to fill the containers below.

Date ____________

The litre jug

You need:
- 5 containers
- litre jug
- water

Compare capacities of containers with a litre

My estimates:

Container	More than the litre jug	About the same as the litre jug	Less than the litre jug
A			
B			
C			
D			
E			

Using a litre jug I found:

Container	More than the litre jug	About the same as the litre jug	Less than the litre jug
A			
B			
C			
D			
E			

Teacher's notes

Choose some containers of different capacities and label them A, B, C, D and E. Estimate whether each container will hold more or less than a litre jug, or the same as a litre jug. Then use a litre jug to check your estimates.

How many in a litre?

- **Measure capacities of different containers**

You need:

- 6 small containers
- litre jug
- water

Teacher's notes

Choose 6 containers which you think hold less than a litre. Then find out how many of each container is needed to fill the litre jug with water. Draw and label each container in the box. Record the number in the circle for that container.

Date ____________________

Counting leaves

Present information in a pictogram

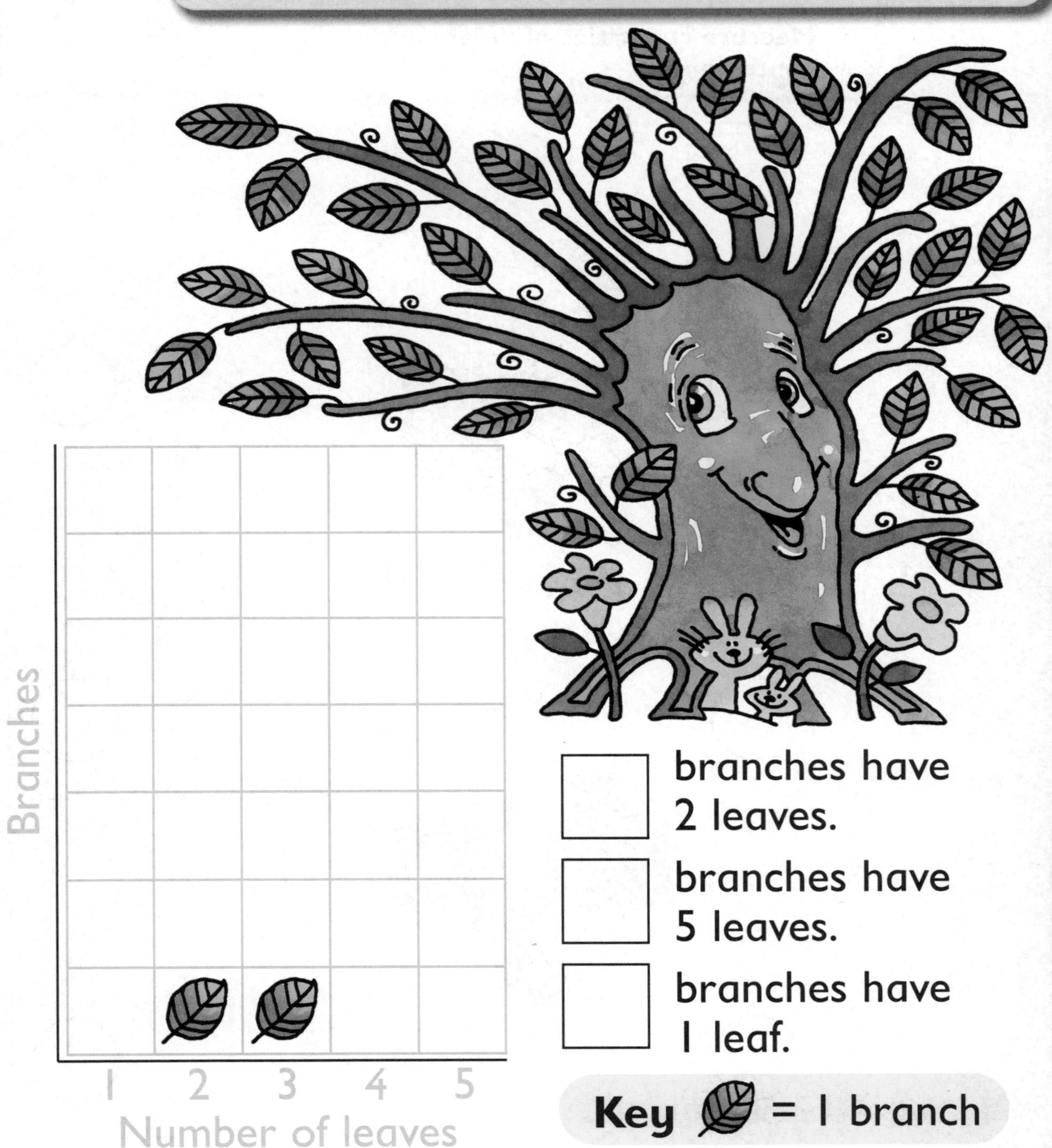

☐ branches have 2 leaves.

☐ branches have 5 leaves.

☐ branches have 1 leaf.

Key 🍃 = 1 branch

Teacher's notes

Count the leaves on each branch. Draw a leaf in the correct column to represent each branch. Then complete the sentences.

Sorting parcels

Use diagrams to sort objects into groups

Teacher's notes

Cross off a parcel. Write its number in the correct sack.

Date ______________________

Fish or flower?

- **Present information in a list, pictogram and table**

You need:
- paper clip and pencil (for the spinner)

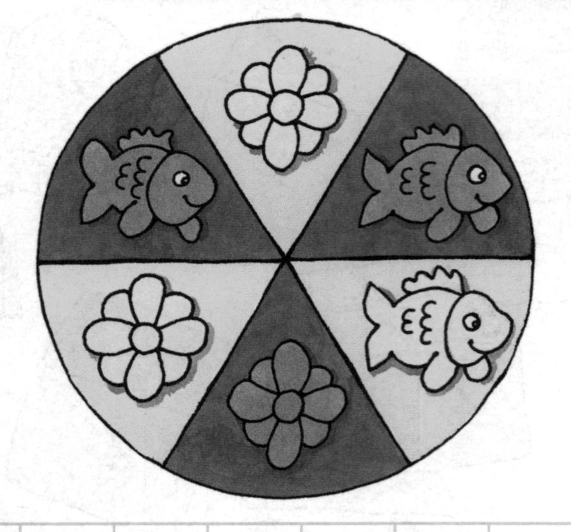

fish							
flower							

Colour
1
2
3
4
5
6
7
8
9
10

The first colour is ☐ .

The last colour is ☐ .

The second colour is ☐ .

There are ☐ fish.

There are ☐ flowers.

Colour	Number
blue	
yellow	

Teacher's notes

Spin the spinner. Write the colour in the list and draw a fish or flower in the pictogram. Do this 10 times. Then complete the table and answer the questions.

Letter train

- Use diagrams to sort objects into groups

You need:

- coloured pencils

B D C B B A C B A A B D C B A

Letter	Number
A	
B	
C	
D	

Number

A B C D

Teacher's notes

Cross off each letter in turn. Write it on the correct train carriage. Then write all the letters in alphabetical order on the track. Complete the table and colour a square for each letter on the block graph.

Date ____________________

Assorted sweets

Use diagrams to sort objects into groups

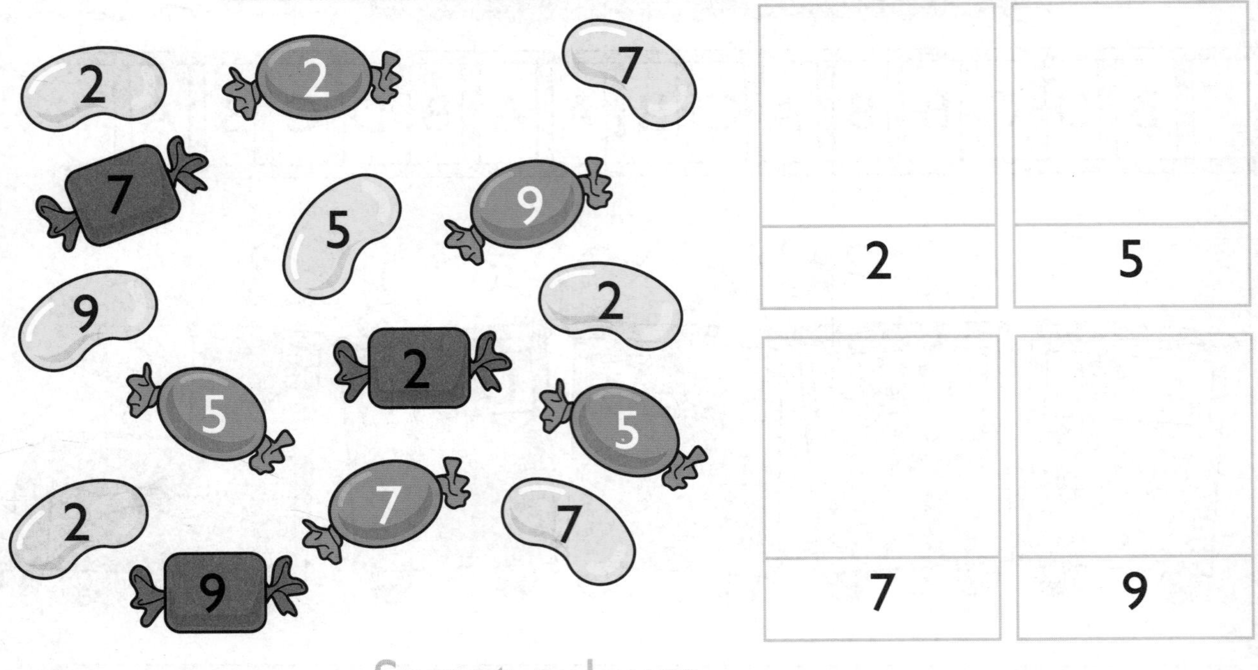

Sweet colours

Red	
Not Red	

Green								
Red								
Yellow								

Key: ◯ stands for 1 sweet

☐ sweets are number 7.

There are ☐ green sweets.

The most common colour is ☐ .

Teacher's notes

Write the sweet numbers in the boxes. Count the red sweets and the sweets that are not red, and complete the table. Draw a circle for each sweet and complete the pictogram.
Then complete the sentences.

Date ____________________

Race against time

Read the time to the hour and half hour

one hour before

one hour after

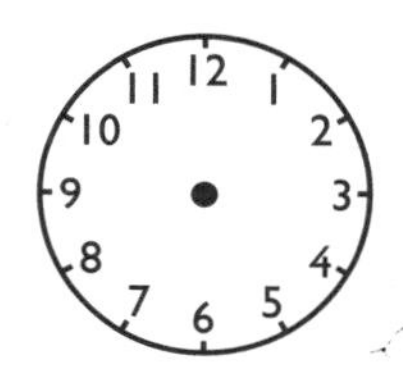

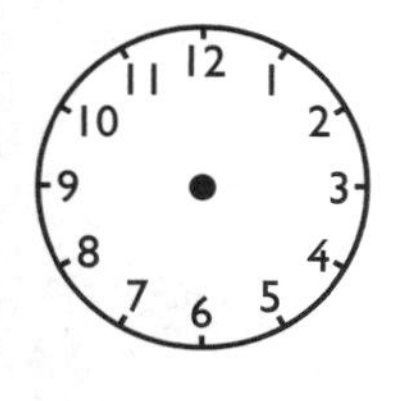

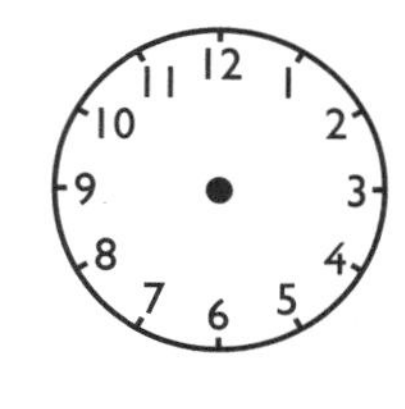

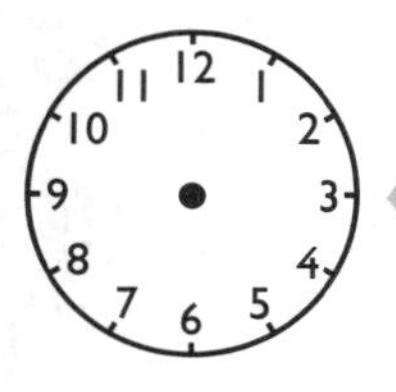
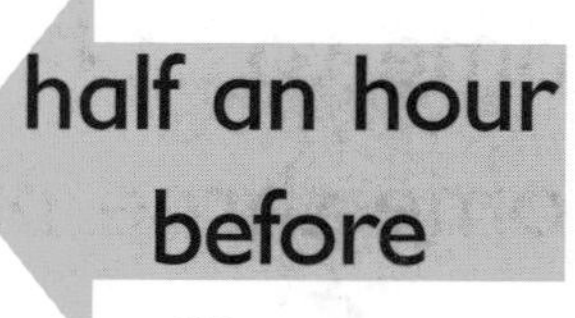

half an hour before

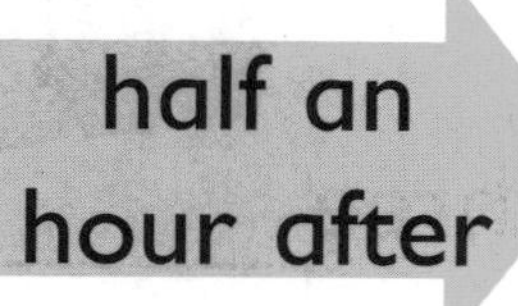

half an hour after

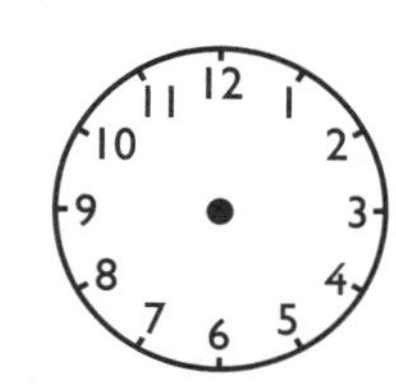

Teacher's notes

Top: Draw times on the clock faces to show one hour before and one hour after the times on the middle clocks.
Bottom: Repeat, but show half an hour before and half an hour after.

Date ____________________

Jay's day

Solve problems about time

Jay gets up at [ ].

Breakfast is half an hour later at [ ].

He leaves the house half an hour later at [ ].

He gets to school half an hour later at [ ].

Lunch is three hours later at [ ].

It is time to go home three and a half hours later at [ ].

How long is Jay at school? [ ]

How long is it between breakfast and lunch? [ ]

Teacher's notes

Top: Write the times that Jay does things in the spaces provided.
Bottom: Look at the times to work out the answers to the questions.

Date ____________________

Monthly moments

Know the order of the months of the year

☐ December	1st January	☐ Febuary

☐ November

☐ October

☐ September

☐ March

☐ April

☐ May

My birthday

Guy Fawkes Night

St Valentine's Day

Christmas Day

New Year's Day

Halloween

My special day

☐ August	☐ July	☐ June

Teacher's notes

Write the ordinal number of each month. Draw a line to join each special day to the month in which it occurs. In the empty box, draw one more special day and join it to its month.

Date ____________________

Capacity problems

- Solve problems about capacity

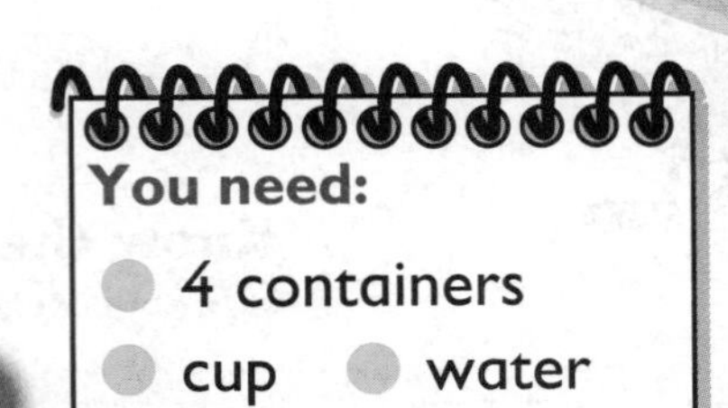

	Container A	Container B	
	☐ cupfuls	☐ cupfuls	
	Container C	Container D	
	☐ cupfuls	☐ cupfuls	

How many cupfuls do container A and container B hold altogether? ☐ ○ ☐ ○ ☐ cupfuls

How many cupfuls do container C and container D hold altogether? ☐ ○ ☐ ○ ☐ cupfuls

How many cupfuls do container A and container C hold altogether? ☐ ○ ☐ ○ ☐ cupfuls

Which container holds more, A or D? ☐

How much more? ☐ ○ ☐ ○ ☐ cupfuls

Teacher's notes

Work in groups. Choose four containers of various capacities and label them A–D. Using a cup and water, find the capacity of each and answer the questions.

Date ____________________

More, the same as, less capacity

- Solve problems about capacity

You need:
- 5 containers
- cup
- sand or beads

Container A holds ☐ cupfuls of ☐

Container B holds ☐ cupfuls of ☐

Container C holds ☐ cupfuls of ☐

Container D holds ☐ cupfuls of ☐

Container E holds ☐ cupfuls of ☐

Container ☐ holds about the same as container ☐

Container ☐ holds less than container ☐

Container ☐ holds less than container ☐

Container ☐ holds more than container ☐

Teacher's notes

Work in groups. Choose five containers of various capacities and label them A–E. Using a cup and a non-standard unit such as sand or beads, find the capacity of each and complete the sentences.

Date ___________________

Planet positions

You need:

- coloured pencils

- **Use words to describe position and direction**

up

down

above

below

left

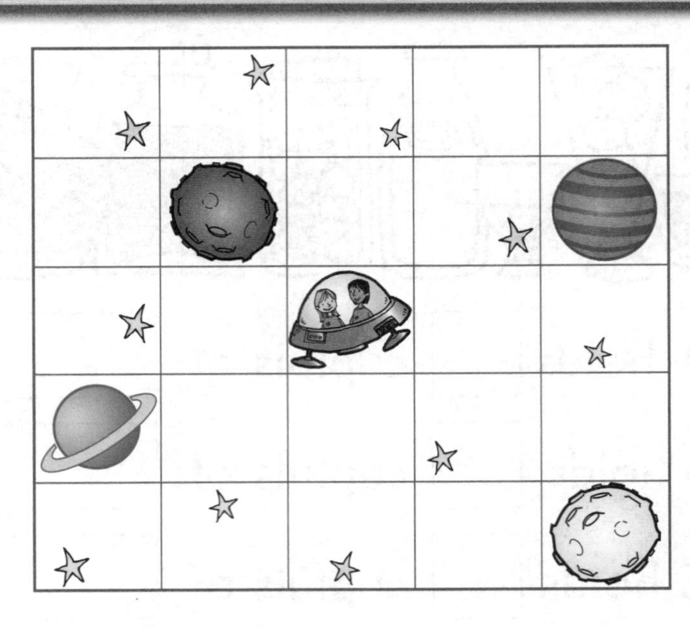

next to

in between

on top of

right

centre

How will you reach …

the red planet? 

the green planet? 

the yellow planet? 

Travel 2 squares up then 2 squares right. Draw a blue planet. 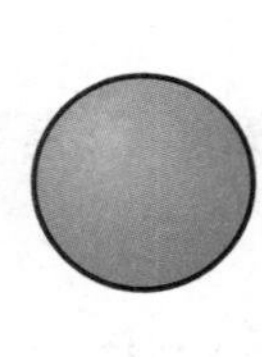

Travel 2 squares down and then 1 square left. Draw an orange planet.

Teacher's notes

You are in the spaceship in the centre of the space grid. Write down directions for reaching some of the planets. Then follow the directions to draw two new planets on the space grid.

Roundabout turns

- Recognise and make quarter turns

Look at the seesaw.  Make a $\frac{1}{4}$ turn to the right. What do you see? ☐

Look at the seesaw. 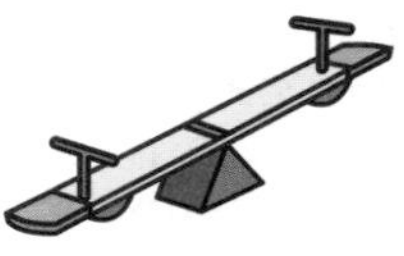 Make a $\frac{1}{4}$ turn to the left. What do you see? ☐

Look at the slide.  Make a $\frac{1}{4}$ turn to the left. What do you see? ☐

Look at the climbing frame. Make a $\frac{1}{4}$ turn to the right. What do you see? ☐

I look at the ☐. I make a $\frac{1}{4}$ turn to the ☐. I can see the .

Teacher's notes

You are on the roundabout in the middle of the park. In the spaces provided, write where you will be facing when you make a quarter turn to the right or a quarter turn to the left.

Date ____________________

Yoyo spending

You need:

- coloured pencils

- **Solve problems about money**

Naomi has 20p.

Ben has 20p.

Amir has 20p.

Ben buys

Amir buys

Naomi buys

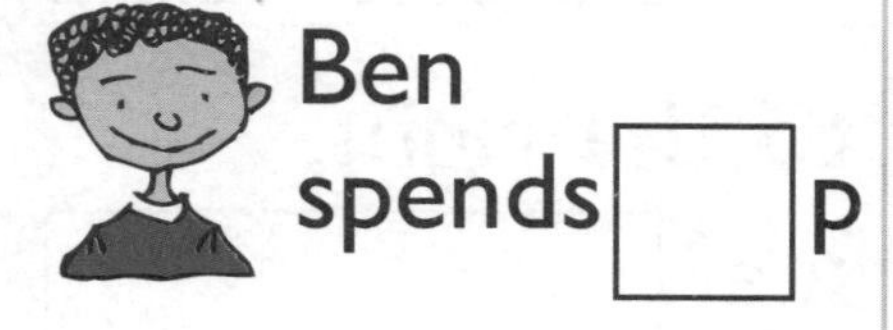

Ben spends ☐ p

Amir spends ☐ p

Naomi spends ☐ p

Teacher's notes

Top: Each child has 20p. Colour the coins so that each one has a different way of making 20p.
Bottom: Each child buys two yoyos. How much does each one spend? Show your working out.

Date ____________________

Coin totals

- Solve problems involving money

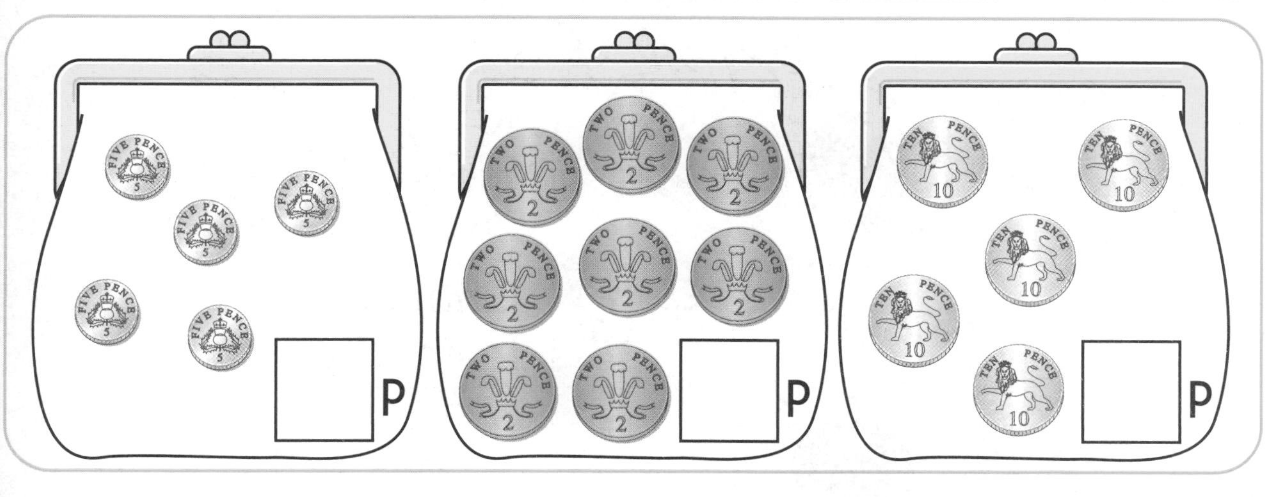

Teacher's notes

Top: Work out how much is in each purse by counting in 2s, 5s or 10s.
Bottom: Work out the pocket money totals – remember to start with the highest value coin.

Date ______________________

Pizza toppings

- **Solve problems about money**

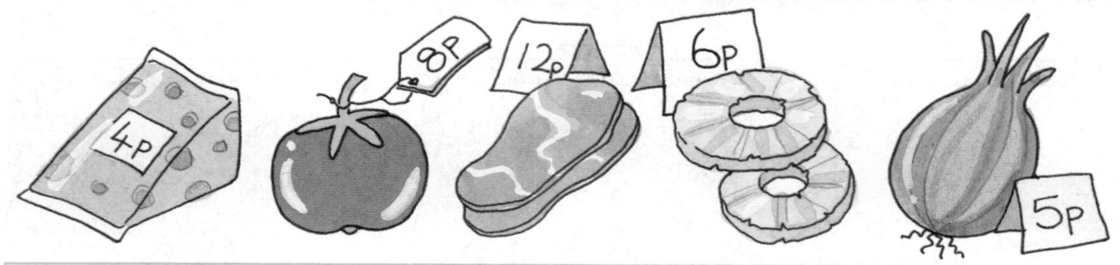

Topping	Total	Change from 20p
	12p	8p

Teacher's notes

In each row, work out the cost of the pizza toppings and the change you will get from 20p. Write the answers in the spaces in the table.

Royal halves and quarters

You need:

- coloured pencils

- **Find $\frac{1}{2}$ and $\frac{1}{4}$ of groups of objects**

Teacher's notes

Top: Count the number of coins in each pile and colour half of them.
Bottom: Count the number of tarts on each plate and colour one quarter of them.

Date ____________________

Cake quarters

You need:

- ruler
- coloured pencils

Find $\frac{1}{2}$, $\frac{1}{4}$ and $\frac{3}{4}$ of shapes

Divide the cake in half. Colour one half of the cake.

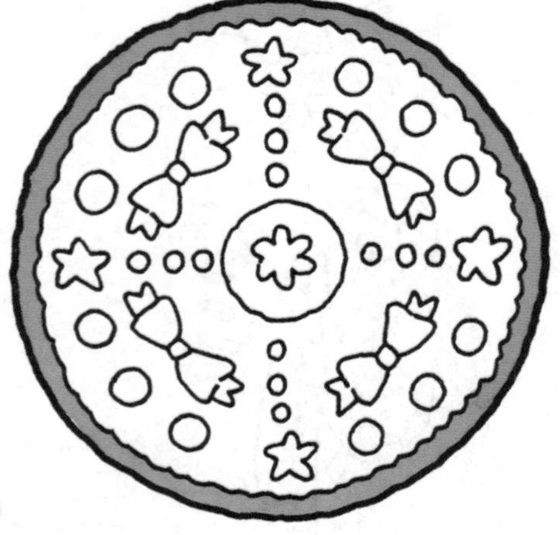

Divide the cake into quarters.Colour one quarter of the cake.

Divide the cake into quarters. Colour three quarters of the cake.

Divide the cake into quarters. Colour one half of the cake.

Teacher's notes

Follow the instructions to divide each cake into halves or quarters, drawing lines to divide each cake. Then colour the fraction of the cake specified.

Date ____________________

Fairground problems

- **Solve word problems**

9 people were on the dodgems. 6 more people joined them.

How many were on the dodgems altogether?

18 people were on the rollercoaster. Tom, Amir and Ellis got off.

How many were left on the rollercoaster?

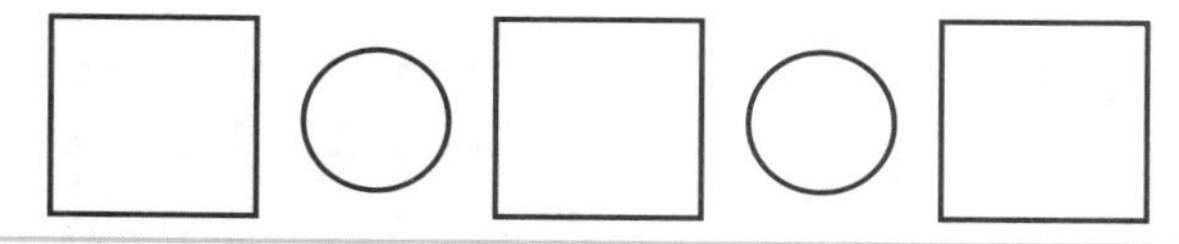

There were 20 toffee apples. Emma bought 1 of them.

How many toffee apples were left?

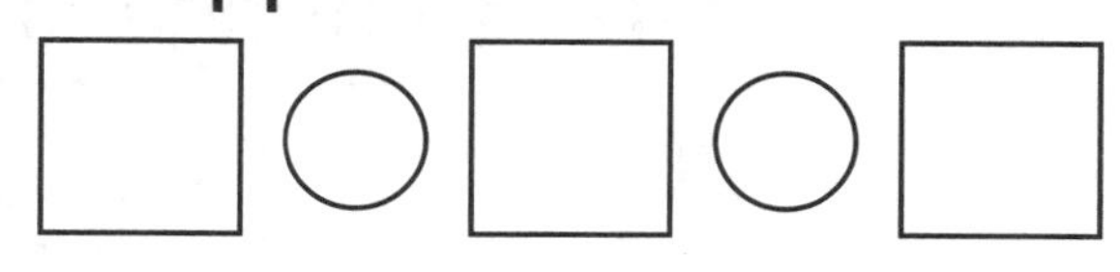

There were 11 prizes on the top shelf. There were 7 more on the bottom shelf.

How many prizes altogether?

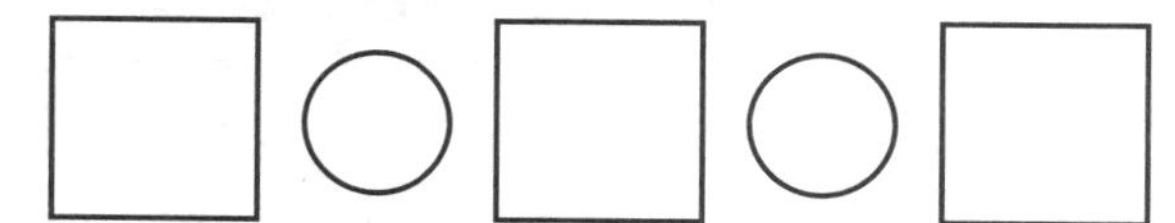

Teacher's notes

Read each word problem. Then write the addition or subtraction calculation in the spaces provided.

Adding up the menu

- Solve word problems

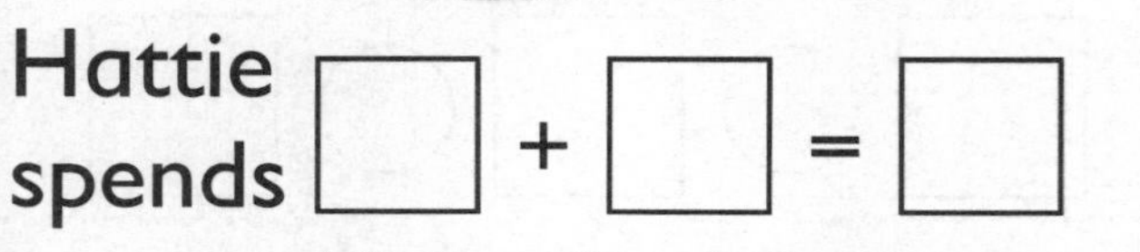

Hattie spends ☐ + ☐ = ☐

Hattie's change is

20p – ☐ = ☐

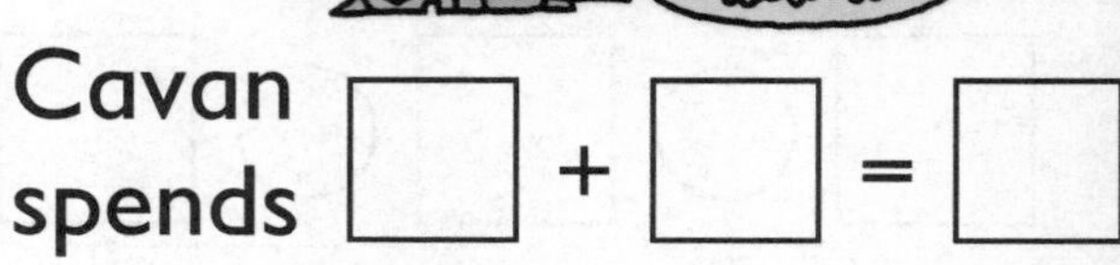

Cavan spends ☐ + ☐ = ☐

Cavan's change is

20p – ☐ = ☐

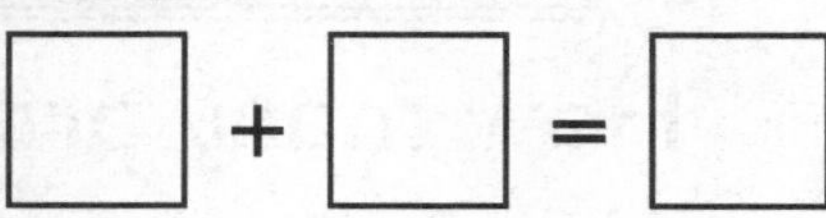

Tom spends ☐ + ☐ = ☐

Tom's change is

20p – ☐ = ☐

Yuko spends ☐ + ☐ = ☐

Yuko's change is

20p – ☐ = ☐

Teacher's notes

Look at the menu. Each child has 20p. First work out how much each child spends.
Then calculate the change each child receives.

Date ____________

Seaside problems

Solve word problems

Samir has found 11 shells.

Ella has 6.
How many shells do they have?

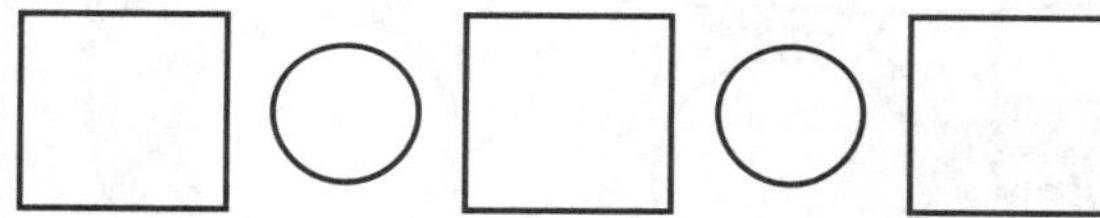

The children have 15 sandwiches.

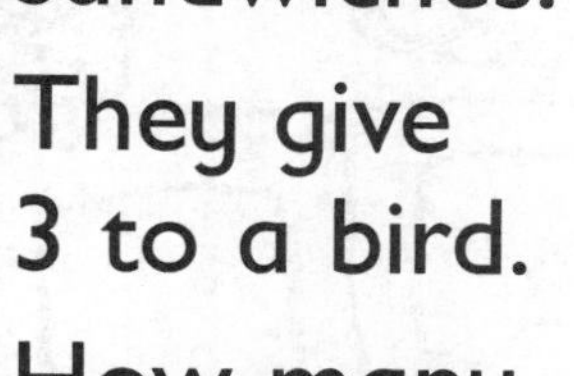

They give 3 to a bird.
How many sandwiches are left?

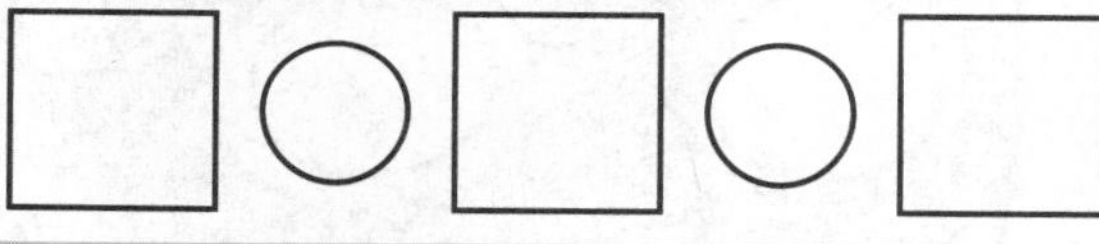

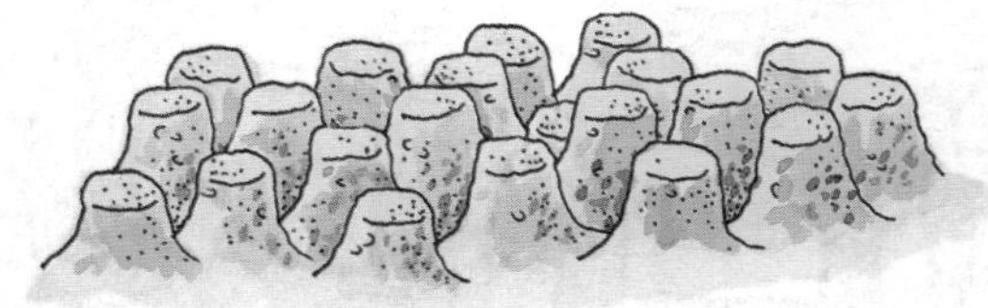

The children made 21 sandcastles.

The sea washed away 5.
How many sandcastles are left?

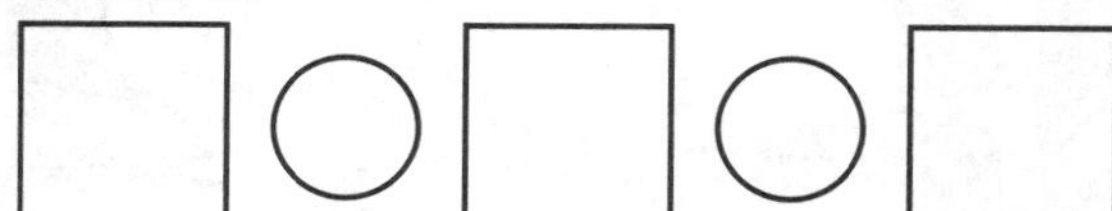

Nadia has counted 11 fish.

Lee has counted 12.

How many fish have they seen altogether?

Teacher's notes

Read each word problem then write the addition or subtraction calculation in the spaces provided.
Extension: Can you write your own addition and subtraction problems using these numbers as your answers? 10, 7, 15 and 22.

Date ____________________

Quilt counting

- Count on or back in 2s, 5s and 10s

Teacher's notes

In each row of the patchwork quilt, count on or back in 2s, 5s or 10s and fill in the missing numbers.

Counting machines

Count on or back in 2s, 5s and 10s

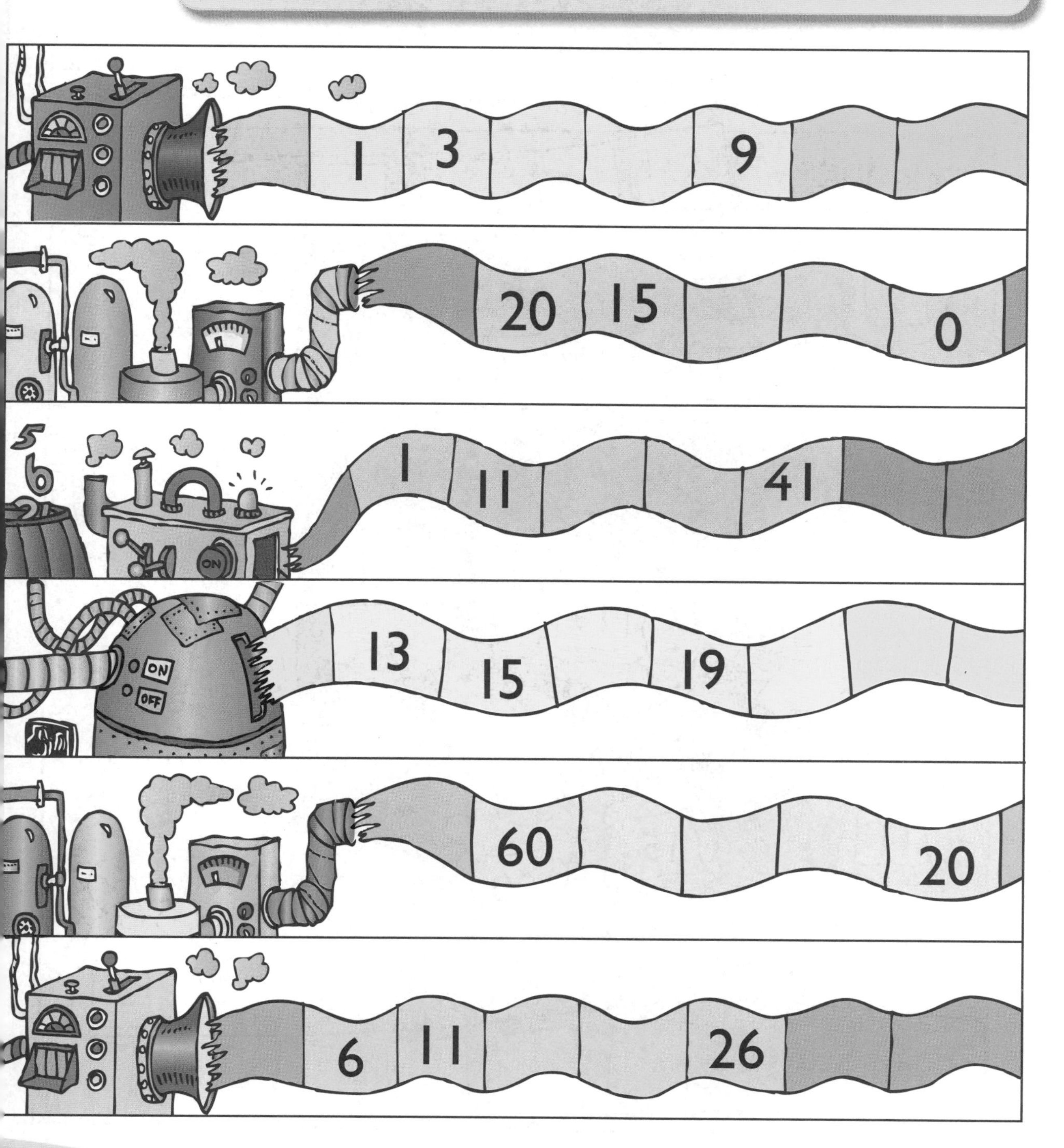

Teacher's notes

Complete the sequence for each counting machine by counting on or back in 2s, 5s or 10s. Write the missing numbers in the spaces provided.

Date ____________________

Odd Jobs and Even Stevens

- **Recognise odd and even numbers to 20**

You need:

- green and blue coloured pencils

Teacher's notes

Colour the shirts of the Odd Jobs team green, and the shirts of the Even Stevens team, blue. Write the numbers for each team in order on their banners.

Date ______________________

Sorting multiples

- Recognise multiples of 2, 5 and 10

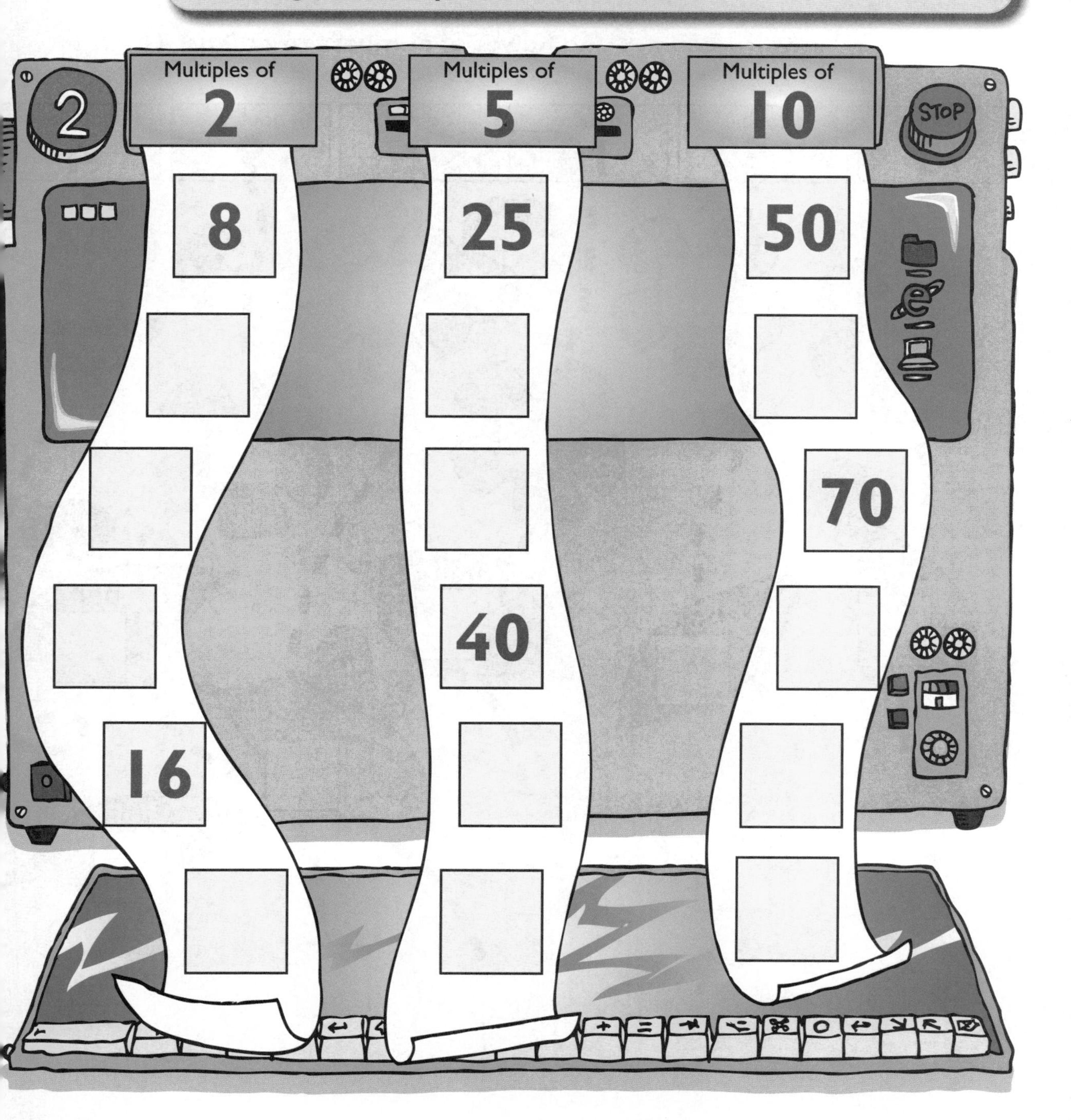

Teacher's notes

The machine is printing multiples of 2, 5 and 10. Write more multiples of each into the spaces on each printout.

Date ____________________

Double and half pathways

Know doubles and halves of numbers to at least 10

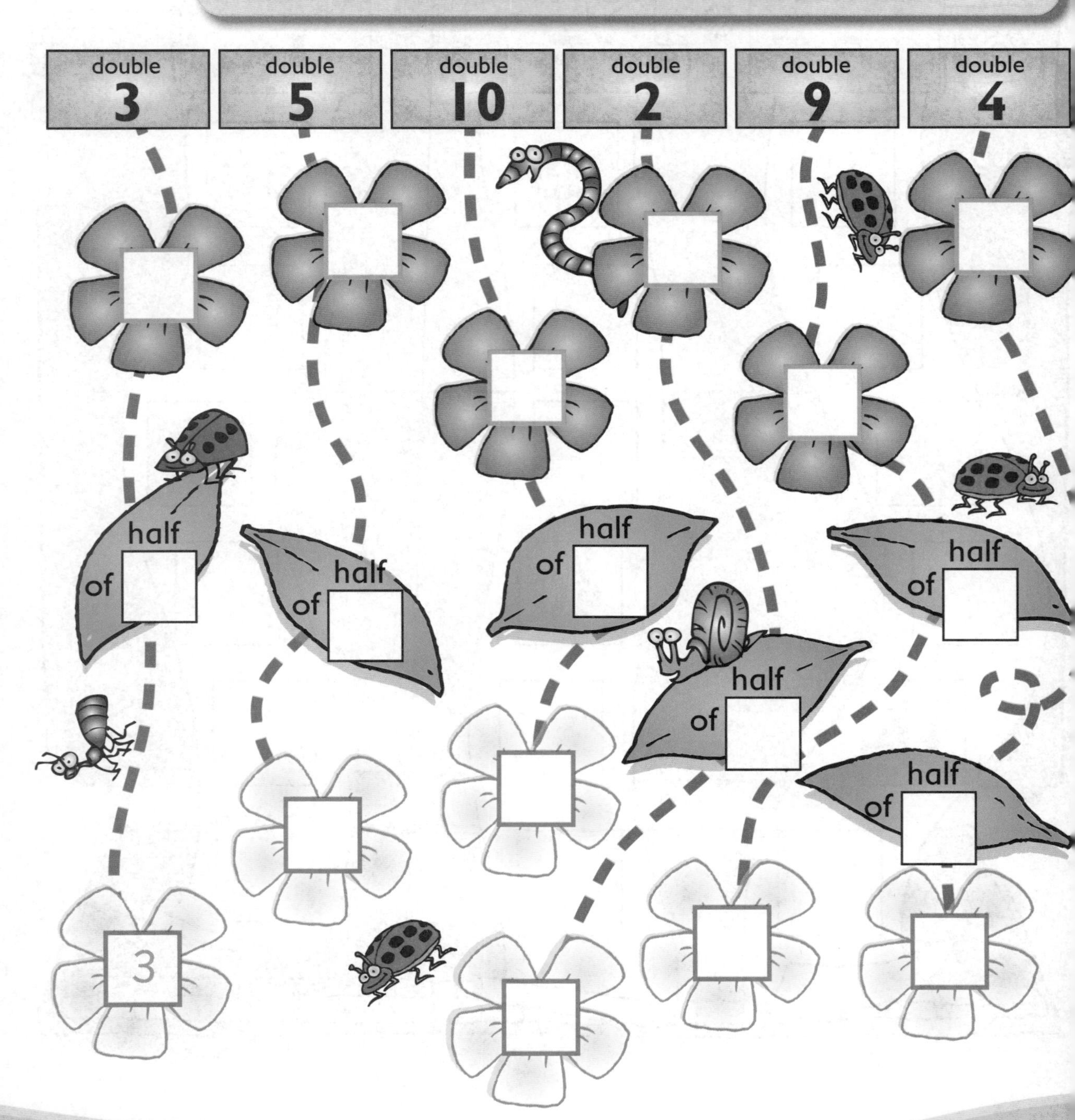

Teacher's notes

Follow the pathways and the instructions to find doubles and halves, writing the correct answers in the boxes.

Date ____________________

Tulip twos

- Solve problems that involve combining groups of 2

You need:

- coloured pencils

5 sets of 2 make 10

9 sets of 2 make

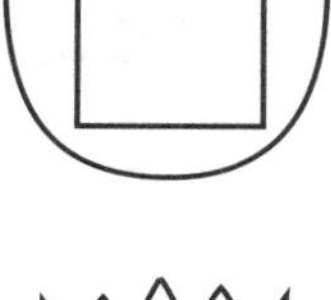

7 sets of 2 make

8 sets of 2 make

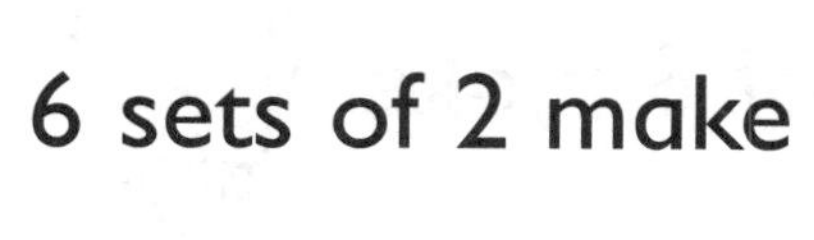

6 sets of 2 make

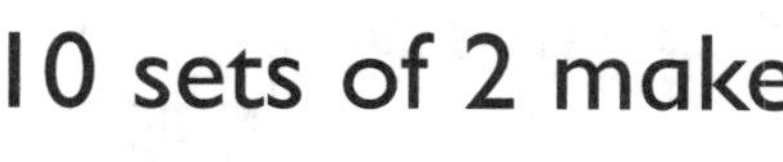

10 sets of 2 make

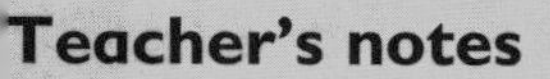

Teacher's notes

Complete each number sentence by writing the correct number in each space. Then match each to the set of tulips showing that number by colouring the answer to match the pots.

Date ____________________

Finger fives

- **Solve problems that involve combining groups of 5**

You need:
- coloured pencils

5 sets of 5 make

9 sets of 5 make

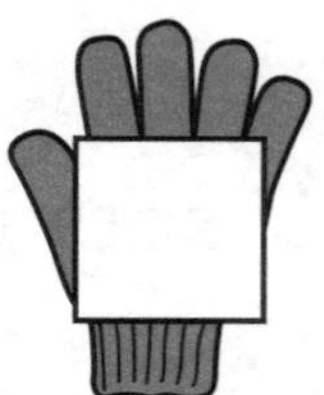

7 sets of 5 make

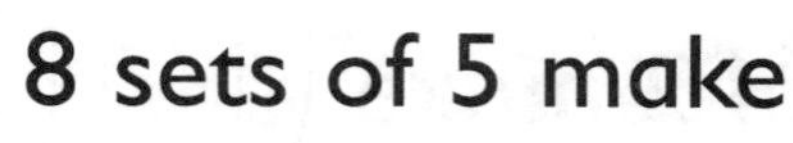

8 sets of 5 make

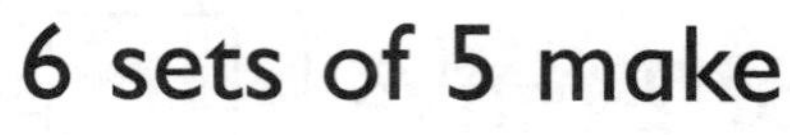

6 sets of 5 make

10 sets of 5 make

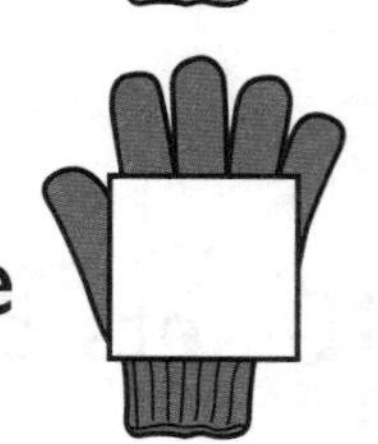

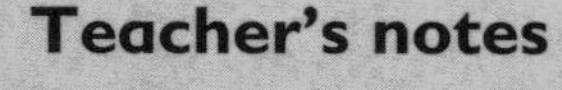

Teacher's notes

Complete each sentence by writing the correct number in each space to show how many fingers there are in each group of gloves. Then match each to the set of gloves showing that number by colouring the gloves to match the answer.

Date ______________________

Terrible teeth tens!

Solve problems that involve combining groups of 10

☐ monsters have

☐ teeth altogether.

☐ monsters have

☐ teeth altogether.

☐ monsters have

☐ teeth altogether.

☐ monsters have

☐ teeth altogether.

☐ monsters have

☐ teeth altogether.

☐ monsters have

☐ teeth altogether.

Teacher's notes

Each monster has 10 terrible teeth! Write how many sets of 10 teeth there are, then work out the number of teeth in each group of monsters, writing the answers in the boxes.

Date ____________________

Sharing shamrocks

Solve problems that involve sharing into equal groups

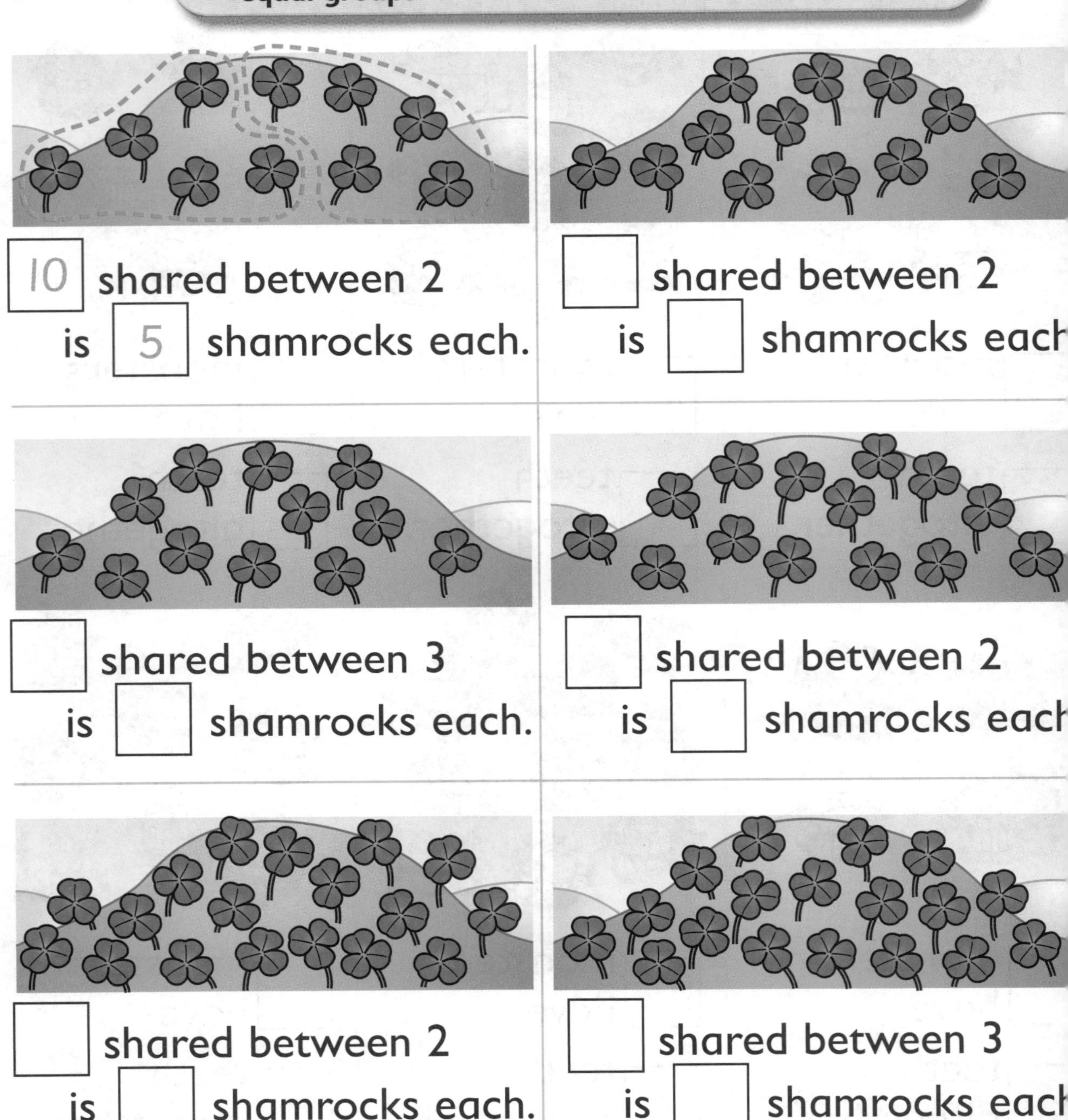

Teacher's notes

In each picture, count the shamrocks and draw lines around them to share them between the number of groups shown. Then complete the sentences by filling in the boxes.

Date ____________________

Solving problems

Solve word problems

There are 5 flowers in each vase.

There are 5 vases.

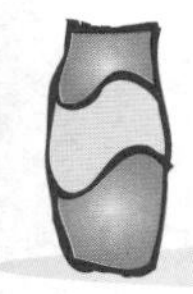
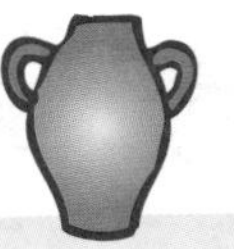

There are [ ] flowers altogether.

There are 16 balloons at the party.

They are shared equally between 4 children.

Each child gets [ ] balloons.

There are 10 apples in each basket.

There are 8 baskets.

There are [ ] apples altogether.

There are 20 cakes on the plate.

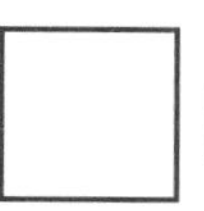

They are shared equally between 5 people.

There are [ ] cakes each.

Teacher's notes

Read each word problem and write your answer in the box.

Maths facts

Number

0 1 2 3 4 5 6 7 8 9 10 11 12 13 14 15 16 17 18 19 20

0	1	2	3	4	5	6	7	8	9	10	11	12	13	14	15	16	17	18	19	20

Addition and subtraction facts to 5

0

0 + 0 = 0   0 – 0 = 0

1

1 + 0 = 1   1 – 1 = 0
0 + 1 = 1   1 – 0 = 1

2

2 + 0 = 2   2 – 2 = 0
1 + 1 = 2   2 – 1 = 1
0 + 2 = 2   2 – 0 = 2

3

3 + 0 = 3   3 – 3 = 0
2 + 1 = 3   3 – 2 = 1
1 + 2 = 3   3 – 1 = 2
0 + 3 = 3   3 – 0 = 3

4

4 + 0 = 4   4 – 4 = 0
3 + 1 = 4   4 – 3 = 1
2 + 2 = 4   4 – 2 = 2
1 + 3 = 4   4 – 1 = 3
0 + 4 = 4   4 – 0 = 4

5

5 + 0 = 5   5 – 5 = 0
4 + 1 = 5   5 – 4 = 1
3 + 2 = 5   5 – 3 = 2
2 + 3 = 5   5 – 2 = 3
1 + 4 = 5   5 – 1 = 4
0 + 5 = 5   5 – 0 = 5

1-100 number square

1	2	3	4	5	6	7	8	9	10
11	12	13	14	15	16	17	18	19	20
21	22	23	24	25	26	27	28	29	30
31	32	33	34	35	36	37	38	39	40
41	42	43	44	45	46	47	48	49	50
51	52	53	54	55	56	57	58	59	60
61	62	63	64	65	66	67	68	69	70
71	72	73	74	75	76	77	78	79	80
81	82	83	84	85	86	87	88	89	90
91	92	93	94	95	96	97	98	99	100

Pairs of numbers that total 10

10 + 0 = 10
9 + 1 = 10
8 + 2 = 10
7 + 3 = 10
6 + 4 = 10
5 + 5 = 10
4 + 6 = 10
3 + 7 = 10
2 + 8 = 10
1 + 9 = 10
0 + 10 = 10

Counting in steps

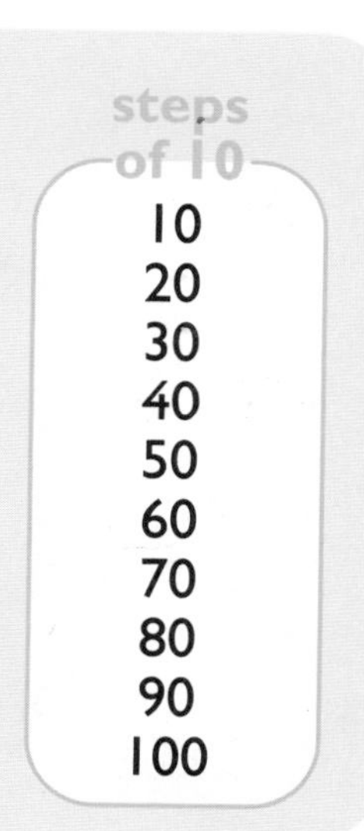

steps of 2	steps of 5	steps of 10
2	5	10
4	10	20
6	15	30
8	20	40
10	25	50
12	30	60
14	35	70
16	40	80
18	45	90
20	50	100

Doubling and halving

1	⟷	2
2	⟷	4
3	⟷	6
4	⟷	8
5	⟷	10
6	⟷	12
7	⟷	14
8	⟷	16
9	⟷	18
10	⟷	20

Shape and space

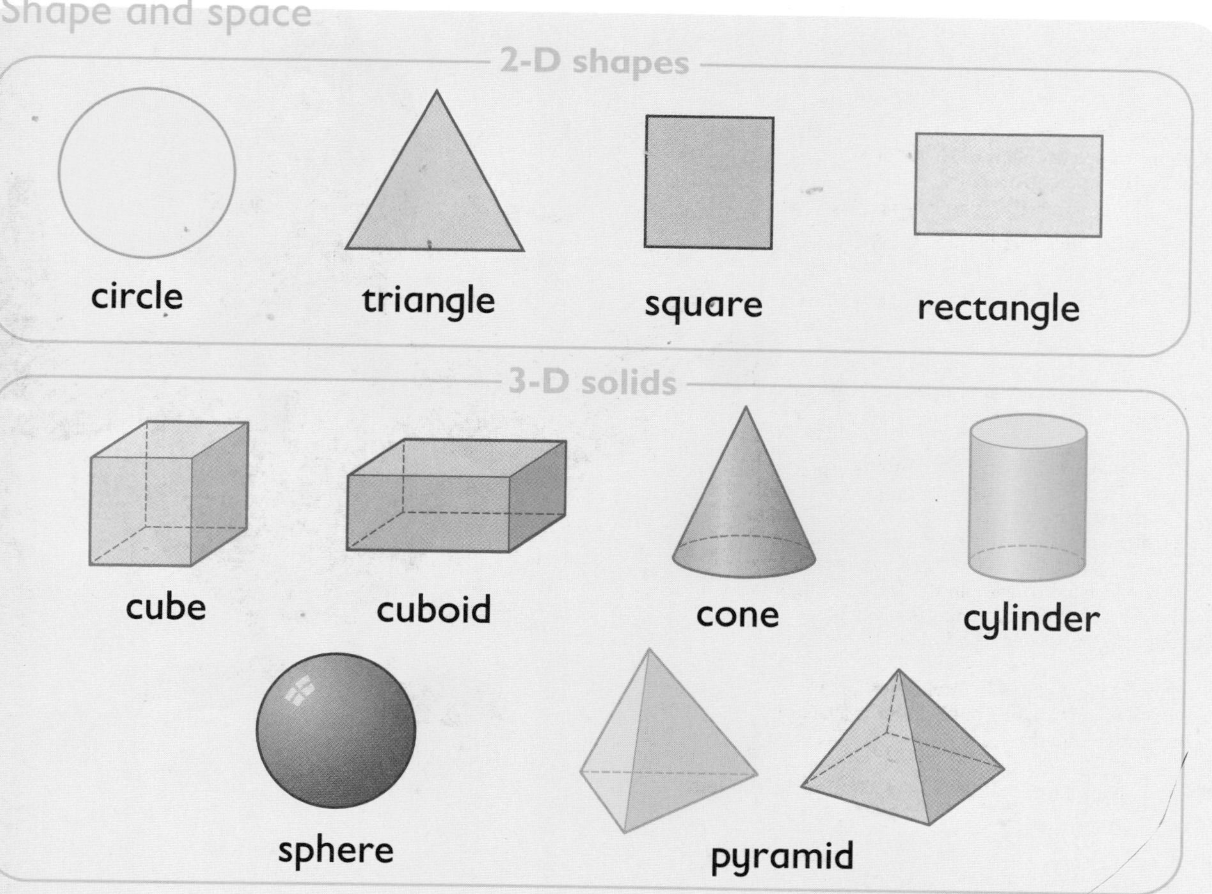

Published by Collins
An imprint of HarperCollins*Publishers*
77-85 Fulham Palace Road
Hammersmith
London
W6 8JB

Browse the complete Collins catalogue at
www.collinseducation.com

10 9

ISBN 978 0 00 722014 4

The authors assert their moral rights to be identified as the authors of this work

British Library Cataloguing in Publication Data
A Catalogue record for this publication is available from the British Library

Printed and bound in Great Britain by Martins the Printers

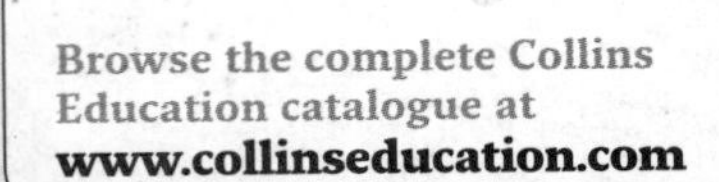